Auditory Processing of Early Language Comprehension Skills

Jean Gilliam DeGaetano

Illustrations by Inky Whalen

Great Ideas for Teaching, Inc. • P.O. Box 444 • Wrightsville Beach, NC 28480-444
www.greatideasforteaching.com

ISBN 1-886143-56-0

Auditory Processing of
Early Language Comprehension Skills

By Jean Gilliam DeGaetano
Illustrations by Inky Whalen

The purpose of these lessons is to increase comprehension of multiple language skills in early learning in the primary grades. While these lessons are primarily designed to improve auditory processing skills, the multiple comprehension skills that are introduced are skills that will appear in their reading comprehension activities later on. By first mastering the various comprehension skills through listening and answering orally, the students should make a smoother transition to developing reading comprehension skills and being able to do independent reading comprehension "seat work."

Observing and interpreting details in a picture is also an essential skill in being successful in completing these lessons. The students should be reminded to constantly look for clues in the pictures. The instructor can expand on the questions by asking if the students knew the answer by looking at the picture or by only hearing the information. While some of the answers can be determined by looking at the picture, other answers can only be found in the story's information.

While looking at the picture, students should listen to a story about the picture. Questions are then asked that separate the story information into specific language comprehension skills, such as; general information comprehension, following directions comprehension, context clues comprehension (to complete the missing words in sentences), time and spatial details comprehension, etc.

Being able to transfer information from skill area to skill area is difficult for some students. Practicing these tasks in auditory processing exercises before doing them in independent work helps students to be more successful in their mastering these comprehension skills.

While these tasks may seem difficult for students with auditory processing weaknesses, learning to complete the tasks in these highly structured lessons will help them learn it is not difficult to separate information in the stories.

If copies of the pages are made prior to working on each lesson, the same pages can be used over again at a later date to practice other skills, such as; doing independent "seat work," learning to write their answers, etc.

Name: _____

Instructor's Worksheet: The purpose of this activity is to help students understand and remember the general meaning and specific details of each story.

Directions: Before beginning, cut out small colored-paper squares to use in the **Following Directions** activities. Each student should be given two squares each of blue, red, yellow and green paper and one copy of the large picture. The instructor will read the story aloud while the students look at their large picture. The students should touch the people and objects in the picture as the story is being read if this aids them in remembering the information. Next, the instructor will read each activity aloud, allowing adequate time for the students to complete each task. When placing a paper square, the students should shield their papers until everyone has finished and then uncover their papers to see if everyone has used the same color and put it in the same place. When answering questions, students should take turns answering the questions aloud. Remembering names is sometimes difficult. The students may need these names reviewed as the questions continue.

Story:

Pam, Chris, Rick and Brad are sitting around a campfire toasting marshmallows. Right now, Brad is the only one holding a stick with marshmallows on it. Pam and Chris are twins. They are sitting beside each other. Rick is the one sitting behind them. Rick's real name is Richard, but he likes to be called by his nickname, Rick. All four of them are on an all-day picnic at the National Park with their school class.

Following Directions:

1. Put a blue square on Brad.
2. Put a red square on each of the twins.
3. Put a green square on the boy who has a nickname.
4. Put a yellow square on someone who is getting ready to toast a couple of marshmallows.
5. Put a green square on something that might be colored green if you were coloring the picture.
6. Put a yellow square on something that might be colored yellow if you were coloring the picture.

General Comprehension:

1. Where are the children?
2. What are they toasting?
3. Point to the boy who has a nickname? What is his nickname?
4. Why do they need a fire?
5. What will they do with the toasted marshmallows?
6. Which children have the same birthday?

Spatial and Time Concepts:

1. Point to the child who has his back turned toward you. What is his name?
2. Point to the person sitting behind the twins. What is his name?
3. Are the twins sitting behind each other or beside each other?
4. Is the fire near the middle of the picture or at one of the sides of the picture?
5. Is this happening at night or during the day?
6. Are they taking turns or toasting their marshmallows at the same time?

Name: _____

Instructor's Worksheet:
The purpose of this activity is to help students understand and remember the general meaning and specific details of each story.

Directions: Before beginning, cut out small colored-paper squares to use in the **Following Directions** activities. Each student should be given two squares each of blue, red, yellow and green paper and one copy of the large picture. The instructor will read the story aloud while the students look at their large picture. The students should touch the people and objects in the picture as the story is being read if this aids them in remembering the information. Next, the instructor will read each activity aloud, allowing adequate time for the students to complete each task. When placing a paper square, the students should shield their papers until everyone has finished and then uncover their papers to see if everyone has used the same color and put it in the same place. When answering questions, students should take turns answering the questions aloud. Remembering names is sometimes difficult. The students may need these names reviewed as the questions continue.

Story:

Cindy, Rick and Chris are in Chris's backyard. When they first came outside, they saw so many insects, worms and spiders that Chris ran back into his house to find an empty jar to collect some of them in. Cindy said, "You can certainly tell that summer is here because there are spiders and insects all over the place." They see caterpillars, spiders, bugs, butterflies, a grasshopper and a baby snake. There is a tiny cocoon attached to a tree limb. They will not touch the cocoon so whatever is inside will be all right. You can tell it is summertime because there are leaves on the trees and flowers blooming all around.

Following Directions:

1. Put a green square on Rick.
2. Put a red square on Chris.
3. Put a yellow square on the insect that can take long jumps.
4. Put a blue square on something they found that has no legs.
5. Put a green square on something that you would color green if you were coloring the picture.

General Comprehension:

1. Where are the children?
2. What did Chris get from his house?
3. How do you know Cindy is not afraid of the baby snake?
4. What will the children do with the jar?
5. What might jump away before they can catch it?
6. What did they find that doesn't have legs?

Spatial and Time Concepts:

1. Spiders have eight legs. How many spiders do you see?
2. Is this happening in the summer or winter? How can you tell?
3. Put a circle around the things that are climbing up something.
4. Put a box around the insect that is climbing down something.
5. Put a dot on the person who is in the middle of the group of children.
6. Is this happening in the daytime or the nighttime?

Name: _____

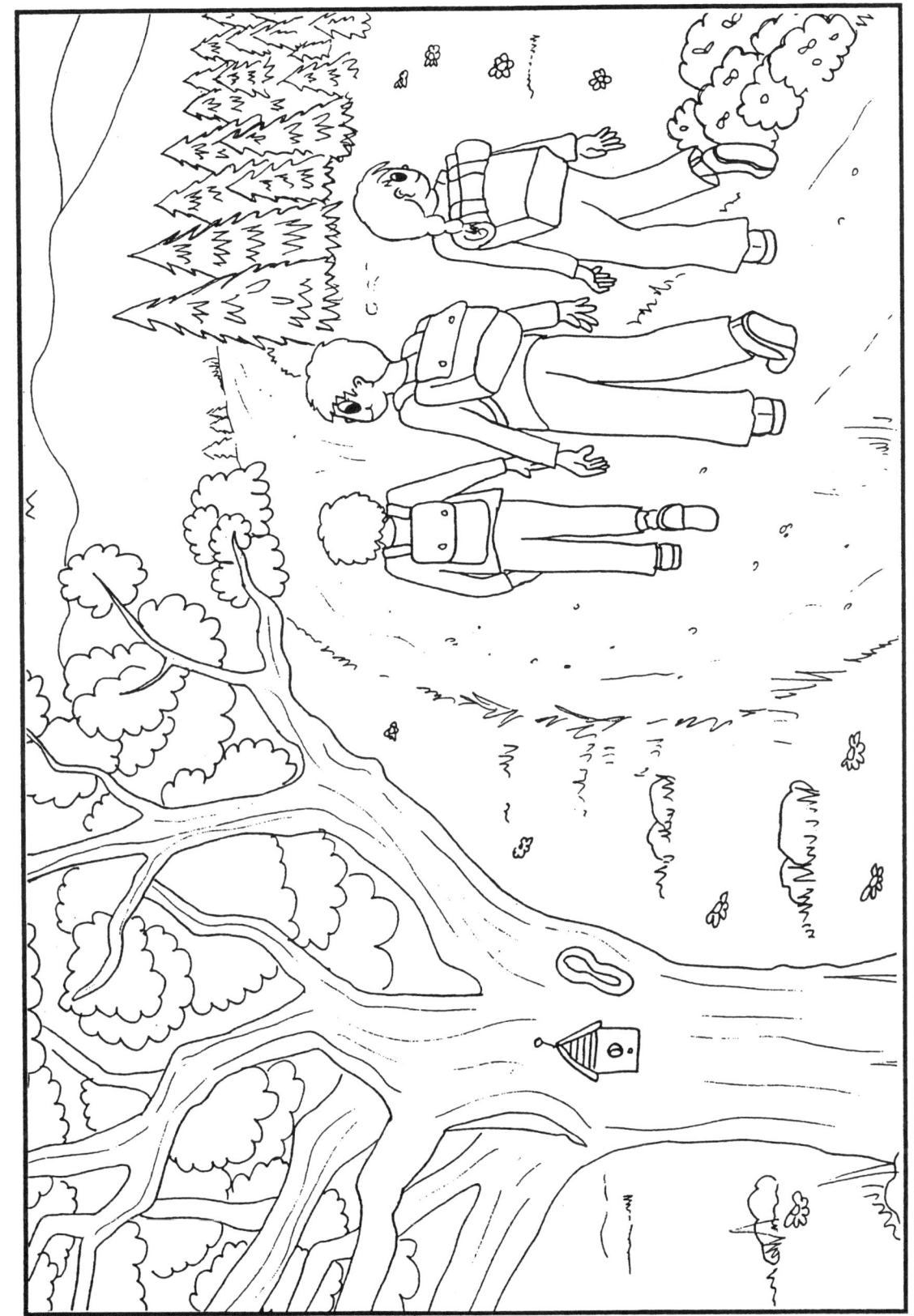

Instructor's Worksheet: The purpose of this activity is to help students understand and remember the general meaning and specific details of each story.

Directions: Before beginning, cut out small colored-paper squares to use in the **Following Directions** activities. Each student should be given two squares each of blue, red, yellow and green paper and one copy of the large picture. The instructor will read the story aloud while the students look at their large picture. The students should touch the people and objects in the picture as the story is being read if this aids them in remembering the information. Next, the instructor will read each activity aloud, allowing adequate time for the students to complete each task. When placing a paper square, the students should shield their papers until everyone has finished and then uncover their papers to see if everyone has used the same color and put it in the same place. When answering questions, students should take turns answering the questions aloud. Remembering names is sometimes difficult. The students may need these names reviewed as the questions continue.

Story:

Cindy, Pam and Chris are taking a hike with Cindy's parents. You do not see her parents because they are walking too far back to be in the picture. You can tell they are walking up a hill. You can see hills and mountains in the distance, so you can guess they are walking near the mountains. They all have backpacks. That is a good clue that they are planning on taking a long hike. It looks like Pam has a rolled mat on her backpack so she has something to sit on when she stops to rest. They probably have water bottles and their favorite food in their backpacks. Chris, the tallest one, has a camera in his backpack.

Following Directions:

1. Put a yellow square on Chris, the tallest child.
2. Put a red square on what Pam plans to sit on to rest.
3. Put a blue square on a mountain.
4. Put a green square on the path they are walking on.
5. Put a blue square on Cindy.
6. Put a green square on something that might be green if you were coloring the picture.

General Comprehension:

1. Where are the children walking? Where are the parents?
2. How do you know they plan to take a long hike?
3. How do you know they are walking up a hill?
4. How do you know Pam doesn't like to sit on the ground?
5. Are they in the city or in the mountains? How do you know?
6. What do they probably have in their backpacks?

Spatial and Time Concepts:

1. Is the tallest child walking ahead of the others?
2. Which two children are walking beside each other?
3. Have they already passed the big tree with a birdhouse on it?
4. Do you see mountains ahead of them or behind them?
5. Are the parents in front of them or behind them?
6. Are the backpacks on the front of their bodies or on their backs?

Auditory Processing of Early
Language Comprehension Skills

Name: _____

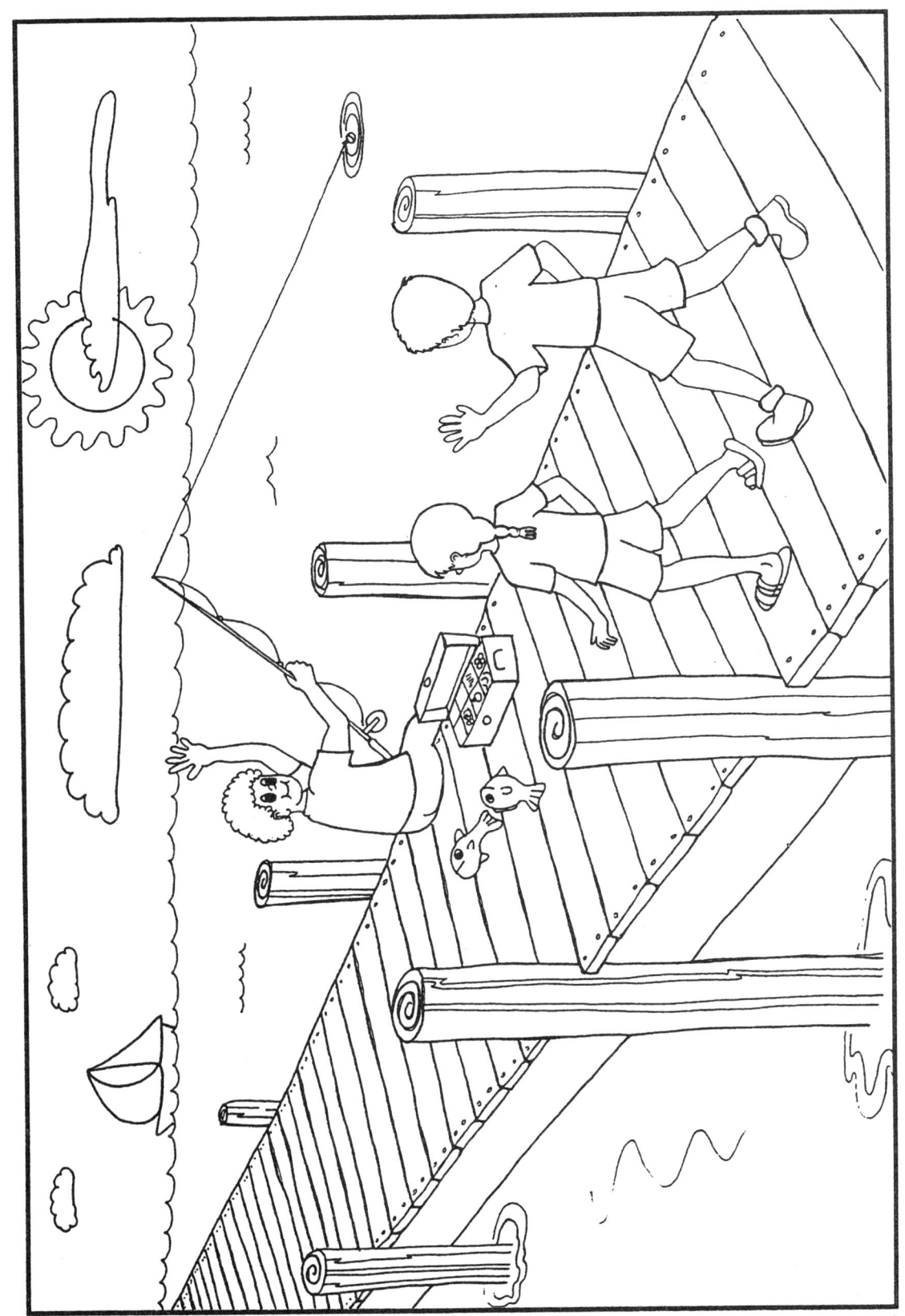

Auditory Processing of Early
Language Comprehension Skills

Great Ideas for Teaching, Inc.

Instructor's Worksheet: The purpose of this activity is to help students understand and remember the general meaning and specific details of each story.

Directions: Before beginning, cut out small colored-paper squares to use in the **Following Directions** activities. Each student should be given two squares each of blue, red, yellow and green paper and one copy of the large picture. The instructor will read the story aloud while the students look at their large picture. The students should touch the people and objects in the picture as the story is being read if this aids them in remembering the information. Next, the instructor will read each activity aloud, allowing adequate time for the students to complete each task. When placing a paper square, the students should shield their papers until everyone has finished and then uncover their papers to see if everyone has used the same color and put it in the same place. When answering questions, students should take turns answering the questions aloud. Remembering names is sometimes difficult. The students may need these names reviewed as the questions continue.

Story:

Chris and Pam are walking on the fishing pier. Their friend Mr. Adams is fishing from the pier. Chris waves to him and he waves back. They can see he has already caught two fish because they see them on the pier. Chris asks Mr. Adams why the fish are on the pier because Mr. Adams usually puts them in a bucket of water. Mr. Adams told Chris he forgot the bucket in his truck. He was hoping he would see Chris so he could ask him to run over to his truck and get the bucket for him. Chris was delighted to help and said he would get the bucket and put water in it so Mr. Adams could catch all the fish he wanted.

Following Directions:

1. Put a red square on the fishing pier.
2. Put a yellow square on the fishing line.
3. Put a blue square on the water.
4. Put a green square on the sailboat.
5. Put a red square on the tackle box Mr. Adams uses when he is fishing.
6. Put a yellow square on one of the fish that has already been caught.

General Comprehension:

1. What is Mr. Adams doing?
2. Where are Pam and Chris walking?
3. How many fish has Mr. Adams caught?
4. What is Chris going to do for Mr. Adams?
5. What will Mr. Adams put in the bucket after Chris puts water in it?

Spatial and Time Concepts:

1. Is the pier above the water or in the water?
2. What holds the pier above the water? Point to these.
3. Do you think Mr. Adams' feet are in the water?
4. Will Chris put water in the bucket before of after he gives it to Mr. Adams?
5. Do you think the sailboat is close to the dock or far away?

Name: _____

Instructor's Worksheet: The purpose of this activity is to help students understand and remember the general meaning and specific details of each story.

Directions: Before beginning, cut out small colored-paper squares to use in the **Following Directions** activities. Each student should be given two squares each of blue, red, yellow and green paper and one copy of the large picture. The instructor will read the story aloud while the students look at their large picture. The students should touch the people and objects in the picture as the story is being read if this aids them in remembering the information. Next, the instructor will read each activity aloud, allowing adequate time for the students to complete each task. When placing a paper square, the students should shield their papers until everyone has finished and then uncover their papers to see if everyone has used the same color and put it in the same place. When answering questions, students should take turns answering the questions aloud. Remembering names is sometimes difficult. The students may need these names reviewed as the questions continue.

Story:

Chris, Pam and Amy are at the beach with their families. They love to play on the beach and swim in the ocean because they live far away where there are no beaches. They have lakes and rivers, but they don't have an ocean. Today they are building a sandcastle. It is going to be very big. They all have on shirts so they will not get sunburned. They know that getting a sunburn can hurt and they are not going to take any chances. When they finish the sandcastle, they will go swimming. Pam is the younger girl and she has braids in her hair. Amy is older and likes to wear her hair loose. Chris is the same age as Pam because they are twins.

Following Directions:

1. Put a blue square on the sandcastle.
2. Put a yellow square on the older girl.
3. Put a yellow square on the thing that can cause a sunburn.
4. Put a green square on something each child is wearing to keep from getting a sunburn.
5. Put a green square on something that can sail.
6. Put a red square on the girl who has braids.

General Comprehension:

1. Where are the children?
2. Do they have an ocean where they live? What do they have?
3. Did they travel a short distance or a long distance to get to the beach?
4. Why are they all wearing shirts?
5. What do you see out in the ocean?
6. What will they do after they build their sandcastle?

Spatial and Time Concepts:

1. Is the time of year winter or summer?
2. Is the weather warm, hot or cold?
3. Are they doing this activity in the daytime or nighttime?
4. Is the sandcastle as tall as Chris?
5. Amy is on her knees. If she stood up, would she be taller or shorter than the sandcastle?
6. Point to the children who are the same age.

Name: _____

Instructor's Worksheet: The purpose of this activity is to help students understand and remember the general meaning and specific details of each story.

Directions: Before beginning, cut out small colored-paper squares to use in the **Following Directions** activities. Each student should be given two squares each of blue, red, yellow and green paper and one copy of the large picture. The instructor will read the story aloud while the students look at their large picture. The students should touch the people and objects in the picture as the story is being read if this aids them in remembering the information. Next, the instructor will read each activity aloud, allowing adequate time for the students to complete each task. When placing a paper square, the students should shield their papers until everyone has finished and then uncover their papers to see if everyone has used the same color and put it in the same place. When answering questions, students should take turns answering the questions aloud. Remembering names is sometimes difficult. The students may need these names reviewed as the questions continue.

Story:

Rick, Pam and Chris have summer jobs on Pam's farm. They are not paying jobs because they are too young to work, but Pam's father does really nice things for them to thank them for helping on the farm. Rick likes to gather watermelons and cucumbers off of the vines. If the watermelons are too heavy, Pam's dad picks them up, but Rick carries all the smaller ones. Pam gathers the eggs. The hens know her and do not mind when she comes into their hen house. Chris carries a small pail of milk to feed all the kittens that live in the barn. He also helps feed the other animals. The children think working on the farm is more fun than playing. In the afternoon, Pam's mother takes the children to the pond for a swim.

Following Directions:

1. Put a yellow square on what hens lay.
2. Put a green square on something that grows on a vine.
3. Put a red square on something kittens love.
4. Look at the picture carefully and put a blue square on a farm tool.
5. Put a green square on something that catches rain water.
6. Put a yellow square on the flower that isn't in the ground.

General Comprehension:

1. What are the children's summer jobs? (Look at the picture for clues.)
2. How does Pam's father thank them for their work?
3. After the children's chores are done, what do they do in the afternoon?
4. Why is Pam the one who gathers the eggs?
5. Who gathers the heavy watermelons?
6. What do the children think is more fun than playing?

Spatial and Time Concepts:

1. The children are standing in front of the barn door. Which child is in the middle?
2. Is the pitchfork inside or outside of the barn?
3. Are the children inside or outside of the barn?
4. Are the children taller or shorter than the rain barrel that catches the rain water?
5. Do the children look like they are about the same age or is one much older?
6. Look at the window. Are the curtains inside or outside of the barn?

Name: _____

Great Ideas for Teaching, Inc.

Instructor's Worksheet: The purpose of this activity is to help students understand and remember the general meaning and specific details of each story.

Directions: Before beginning, cut out small colored-paper squares to use in the **Following Directions** activities. Each student should be given two squares each of blue, red, yellow and green paper and one copy of the large picture. The instructor will read the story aloud while the students look at their large picture. The students should touch the people and objects in the picture as the story is being read if this aids them in remembering the information. Next, the instructor will read each activity aloud, allowing adequate time for the students to complete each task. When placing a paper square, the students should shield their papers until everyone has finished and then uncover their papers to see if everyone has used the same color and put it in the same place. When answering questions, students should take turns answering the questions aloud. Remembering names is sometimes difficult. The students may need these names reviewed as the questions continue.

Story:

Chris, Pam and Rick are playing hide and seek with their friends. They decided to hide in Pam's mother's garden. The flower bushes, ferns and plants with large leaves are so thick and full that the children did not think anyone could find them. Pam's dog followed them and Pam told it not to bark. They soon discovered that lots of bugs, caterpillars and butterflies were in those same bushes. Rick is hiding behind the log. Chris is behind the tree. Pam is hiding behind the bushes with her dog. They are not making a sound! Even the insects, the baby bird and Pam's dog are not making any noise. Do you think they picked a good place to hide?

Following Directions:

1. Put a yellow square on something that tells you it is not a rainy day.
2. Put a blue square on the child who owns the dog.
3. Put a red square on something that is crawling on a log.
4. Put an green square on something that can fly.
5. Put a blue square on something that has a trunk.
6. Put a yellow square on something that is in a little house.

General Comprehension:

1. What game are the children playing?
2. Where did they think would be a great place to hide?
3. Why did Pam tell her dog not to bark?
4. What other living things are in the bushes besides the children?
5. Why are they not making any noise?
6. Are any of the children afraid of bugs?

Spatial and Time Concepts:

1. Are the children playing in the daytime or the nighttime?
2. How do you know it is summertime?
3. Are the children in the bushes or in front of them?
4. Point to the things on the tree that are smaller than the birdhouse.
5. Point to the person who is hiding next to the dog.
6. Point to the things that are flying above the plants.

Auditory Processing of Early
Language Comprehension Skills

Name: _____

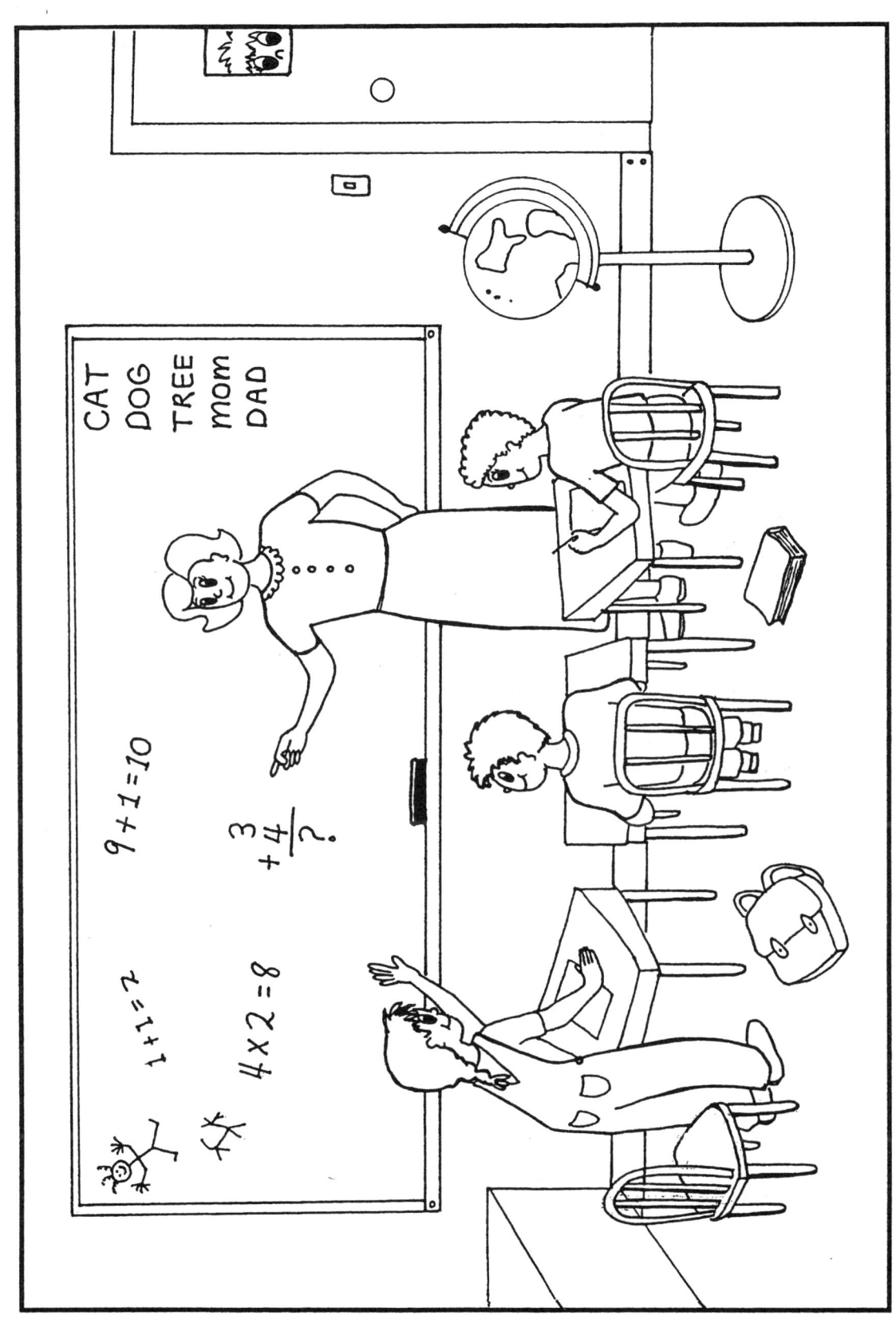

Auditory Processing of Early
Language Comprehension Skills

Great Ideas for Teaching, Inc.

Instructor's Worksheet: The purpose of this activity is to help students understand and remember the general meaning and specific details of each story.

Directions: Before beginning, cut out small colored-paper squares to use in the **Following Directions** activities. Each student should be given two squares each of blue, red, yellow and green paper and one copy of the large picture. The instructor will read the story aloud while the students look at their large picture. The students should touch the people and objects in the picture as the story is being read if this aids them in remembering the information. Next, the instructor will read each activity aloud, allowing adequate time for the students to complete each task. When placing a paper square, the students should shield their papers until everyone has finished and then uncover their papers to see if everyone has used the same color and put it in the same place. When answering questions, students should take turns answering the questions aloud. Remembering names is sometimes difficult. The students may need these names reviewed as the questions continue.

Story:

Mrs. Tuttle is a second-grade teacher. Each day after school she helps three students catch up on work they missed when they were absent. Everyone loves staying after school for extra work because after they finish, Mrs. Tuttle has a cookie and juice party for them. All the students love Mrs. Tuttle. They wish she could move to third grade so they could have her for a teacher again next year. Today they are working on math. Pam must know the answer for the math problem because she has raised her hand. Chris is sitting in the middle and Rick is sitting near the globe.

Following Directions:

1. Put a red square on the math problem they are working on.
2. Put a yellow square on the person who knows the answer.
3. Put a green square on the person who is helping the students.
4. Put a blue square on Chris.
5. Put a red square on the blackboard eraser.
6. Put a yellow square on the globe.

General Comprehension:

1. Which two people are not sitting?
2. Why are these students staying after school?
3. Are they happy to be getting extra help? How can you tell?
4. What will they enjoy after they finish their work?
5. What subject are they working on today?
6. What do the children wish would happen next year?

Spatial and Time Concepts:

1. How many students does Mrs. Tuttle help at one time?
2. Does Mrs. Tuttle hold her special class before or after the regular school day?
3. Do the students have juice and cookies before or after they finish their work?
4. Point to the person who is taller than everyone else.
5. Is the globe next to Pam or next to one of the boys?
6. Is Mrs. Tuttle standing in front of the children or behind the children?

Name: _____

Auditory Processing of Early
Language Comprehension Skills

Great Ideas for Teaching, Inc.

Instructor's Worksheet: The purpose of this activity is to help students understand and remember the general meaning and specific details of each story.

<u>Directions:</u> Before beginning, cut out small colored-paper squares to use in the **Following Directions** activities. Each student should be given two squares each of blue, red, yellow and green paper and one copy of the large picture. The instructor will read the story aloud while the students look at their large picture. The students should touch the people and objects in the picture as the story is being read if this aids them in remembering the information. Next, the instructor will read each activity aloud, allowing adequate time for the students to complete each task. When placing a paper square, the students should shield their papers until everyone has finished and then uncover their papers to see if everyone has used the same color and put it in the same place. When answering questions, students should take turns answering the questions aloud. Remembering names is sometimes difficult. The students may need these names reviewed as the questions continue.

Story:

Today is the first day of school. Rick is in second grade. This morning he was really scared that he would not be able to find his classroom. His older friend Sam told him not to worry because he would walk him to class. You see they are walking to Rick's class. Sam told him, "This will be easy to remember because you are the door next to the stairs." It looks like Rick is bringing a surprise to show his teacher. It is a butterfly in a jar. After the children see it, he will ask the teacher if they can open the window and set the butterfly free. Look at the clock. It is nine o'clock in the morning.

Following Directions:

1. Put a blue square on the boy who is in second grade.
2. Put a yellow square on Rick's older friend.
3. Put a red square on the door of Rick's classroom.
4. Put a green square on something that tells the students when they are late.
5. Put a red square on the boy who is at the top of the stairs.
6. Put a green square on the surprise Rick is taking to his class.

General Comprehension:

1. Where are Rick and Sam?
2. Why was Rick scared?
3. How did Sam make his friend feel better?
4. Is Rick still scared? Explain.
5. What did Sam tell Rick about remembering where his class is?
6. What will Rick do with the butterfly after the students see it?

Spatial and Time Concepts:

1. What time is it now?
2. Is Rick late for class?
3. Is the door to Rick's classroom beside or in front of the stairs?
4. Are the other children walking up or down the stairs?
5. Is Sam taller than Rick or is Rick taller than Sam?
6. Is this happening in the morning or the afternoon?

Name: _____

Auditory Processing of Early
Language Comprehension Skills

Great Ideas for Teaching, Inc.

Instructor's Worksheet: The purpose of this activity is to help students understand and remember the general meaning and specific details of each story.

Directions: Before beginning, cut out small colored-paper squares to use in the **Following Directions** activities. Each student should be given two squares each of blue, red, yellow and green paper and one copy of the large picture. The instructor will read the story aloud while the students look at their large picture. The students should touch the people and objects in the picture as the story is being read if this aids them in remembering the information. Next, the instructor will read each activity aloud, allowing adequate time for the students to complete each task. When placing a paper square, the students should shield their papers until everyone has finished and then uncover their papers to see if everyone has used the same color and put it in the same place. When answering questions, students should take turns answering the questions aloud. Remembering names is sometimes difficult. The students may need these names reviewed as the questions continue.

Story:

Randy can play a guitar. Actually, he plays it very, very well and he can sing as well as lots of people who are famous. The other kids love to sit around and listen to him. He knows all the most popular songs. Randy is going to be in a special talent show in two weeks. The person who wins first prize will get a chance to be on television. He has been practicing for two hours each day, getting ready for the show. He doesn't mind all the kids in the neighborhood coming to listen to him. He has a special place to practice. It is under one of his favorite trees behind his house. There is a hill behind the big tree. He has put out logs for seats and pretends it is a big place to give concerts.

Following Directions:

1. Put a green square on the hill.
2. Put blue squares on the things that are used for seats.
3. Put a yellow square on the guitar.
4. Put a yellow square on the thing that lets you know it is daytime.
5. Put a green square on something you would color green if you were coloring the picture.
6. Put a red square on the largest limb you see on the tree.

General Comprehension:

1. What instrument does Randy play?
2. Why is he practicing?
3. What does he hope to win?
4. What will the winner get a chance to be on?
5. Why did he put logs under the tree?

Spatial and Time Concepts:

1. What clues tell you it is summertime?
2. What is behind the tree?
3. Are the other children sitting in front of or behind Randy?
4. Does Randy do his practicing in the daytime or the nightime?
5. Where is everyone?
6. Has the talent show happened yet? When is it?

Auditory Processing of Early
Language Comprehension Skills

Name: _____

Instructor's Worksheet: The purpose of this activity is to help students understand and remember the general meaning and specific details of each story.

Directions: Before beginning, cut out small colored-paper squares to use in the **Following Directions** activities. Each student should be given two squares each of blue, red, yellow and green paper and one copy of the large picture. The instructor will read the story aloud while the students look at their large picture. The students should touch the people and objects in the picture as the story is being read if this aids them in remembering the information. Next, the instructor will read each activity aloud, allowing adequate time for the students to complete each task. When placing a paper square, the students should shield their papers until everyone has finished and then uncover their papers to see if everyone has used the same color and put it in the same place. When answering questions, students should take turns answering the questions aloud. Remembering names may be difficult. The students may need these names reviewed as the questions continue.

Story:

The ice cream man has his ice cream stand set up in the park. Pam and Chris are the two children standing closest to the stand. Ann wanted a vanilla ice cream cone but Chris wants a chocolate fudgsicle. They are brother and sister. They live very close to the park so it is just a short walk from their house to the ice cream stand. The boy who is running to the stand is another friend of theirs. He lives in their neighborhood. His name is Bob. It looks like the boy on the left is just walking by the stand and is not planning to buy ice cream. It is a warm, sunny day so the ice cream man has an umbrella to give him shade. The sun will probably make their ice cream melt if they do not eat it quickly.

Auditory Processing for General Comprehension:

1. Where is the ice cream stand?
2. How far away do the children live?
3. What kind of day is it?
4. Does everyone in the picture want to buy ice cream? Explain.
5. Do Pam and Chris like the same kind of ice cream? Explain.

Auditory Processing for Following Directions:

1. Draw a circle on the man who sells ice cream.
2. Put a line over the person who likes vanilla ice cream.
3. Put an "X" on the person who does not plan to buy ice cream.
4. Put a red square on something that will shade the ice cream stand.
5. Put a yellow square on something that will make the ice cream melt.

Auditory Processing and Sentence Completion:

1. Pam bought a vanilla _____.
2. Chris bought a chocolate _____.
3. The sun will make the ice cream _____.
4. The boy on the left does not look like he wants _____.
5. The umbrella will shade the _____.

Auditory Processing and Remembering Specific Information:

1. Who is eating a vanilla ice cream cone?
2. Who will eat a chocolate fudgsicle?
3. Where is the ice cream stand?
4. Which two children are brother and sister? Name them.
5. Do you remember the name of their friend who is running to the ice cream stand?

Name: _____

Instructor's Worksheet: The purpose of this activity is to help students understand and remember the general meaning and specific details of each story.

<u>Directions:</u> Before beginning, cut out small colored-paper squares to use in the **Following Directions** activities. Each student should be given two squares each of blue, red, yellow and green paper and one copy of the large picture. The instructor will read the story aloud while the students look at their large picture. The students should touch the people and objects in the picture as the story is being read if this aids them in remembering the information. Next, the instructor will read each activity aloud, allowing adequate time for the students to complete each task. When placing a paper square, the students should shield their papers until everyone has finished and then uncover their papers to see if everyone has used the same color and put it in the same place. When answering questions, students should take turns answering the questions aloud. Remembering names may be difficult. The students may need these names reviewed as the questions continue.

Story:

The boys in the neighborhood skate together every afternoon in the summertime when school is out. Some have skateboards and some have roller skates. They usually race to the end of the street. Some days they just skate along without racing, but when they get three or four boys together, they usually have a lot of races. When they get hot and tired, they go to one of their homes for cold water. Sometimes one of the mothers will offer them cookies or Popsicles. Today, Ted's mother has invited them over. Ted is the skater wearing the helmet. He told the other boys that his mom has lemonade and cookies for them later.

Auditory Processing for General Comprehension:

1. How many boys are skating together today?
2. Where do they usually end the race?
3. What do they do when they all get thirsty?
4. What time of year is it?
5. What makes you think they all get along well together?

Auditory Processing for Following Directions:

1. Put a red square on the youngest child.
2. Put a line under the boy whose mother has something for them later.
3. Circle something that can fly and sting.
4. Put a blue star on each boy who is using a skateboard.
5. Put a green square on a piece of safety equipment.

Auditory Processing and Sentence Completion:

1. All the boys get together in the summertime to _____.
2. Two of the boys are on skateboards and two are on _____.
3. When they race, they skate to the end of the _____.
4. When they get thirsty, they go to someone's _____.
5. When Ted skates, his mother makes him wear a _____.

Auditory Processing and Remembering Specific Information:

1. What is Ted wearing to keep him safe?
2. Whose house are they going to later?
3. What time of year is it?
4. What is Ted's mother going to serve the boys?
5. What insect in the picture can both fly and sting?

Name: _____

Instructor's Worksheet: The purpose of this activity is to help students understand and remember the general meaning and specific details of each story.

<u>Directions:</u> Before beginning, cut out small colored-paper squares to use in the **Following Directions** activities. Each student should be given two squares each of blue, red, yellow and green paper and one copy of the large picture. The instructor will read the story aloud while the students look at their large picture. The students should touch the people and objects in the picture as the story is being read if this aids them in remembering the information. Next, the instructor will read each activity aloud, allowing adequate time for the students to complete each task. When placing a paper square, the students should shield their papers until everyone has finished and then uncover their papers to see if everyone has used the same color and put it in the same place. When answering questions, students should take turns answering the questions aloud. Remembering names may be difficult. The students may need these names reviewed as the questions continue.

Story:

Gary is babysitting this afternoon with the Smith boys. They are not babies so he really is not babysitting, but people just seem to call it that. The Smith boys are Will and Bill. Their mother is Jill and their father is Gill. Everyone in the family has a rhyming name. Gary is also taking care of their dog. Her name is Lil. Gary is starting to swing Will around in a circle. Bill is hanging by his hands from a tree limb and Lil is trying to jump and catch his feet. The boys love to have Gary stay with them when their mother goes shopping because he always plays with them. Some of their babysitters just sit and watch them play. You can see several things in the picture that let you know it is summer. You see butterflies, leaves on the tree, and everyone in short sleeves.

Auditory Processing for General Comprehension:

1. Why is Gary over at the Smith house?
2. Are the boys babies?
3. Where is Mrs. Smith?
4. What is different about the names of the people in the Smith family?
5. Why do the children like to have Gary babysit them?

Auditory Processing for Following Directions:

1. Put a red square on Lil.
2. Put a yellow square on the oldest person in the picture.
3. Two people in the picture are brothers. Draw a line from one to the other.
4. Circle something that swings back and forth.
5. Put a line under everything that can fly.

Auditory Processing and Sentence Completion:

1. Today Gary is _____.
2. The Smith boys are named Will and _____.
3. The Smith family all have rhyming first _____.
4. They are playing in the _____.
5. Bill is hanging from a _____.

Auditory Processing and Remembering Specific Information:

1. What is Mrs. Smith's first name?
2. Which babysitter do the Smith children like best?
3. What are the Smith boys' first names?
4. What is the name of their dog?
5. Is it summertime or wintertime?

Auditory Processing of Early
                                                                              Language Comprehension Skills

Name: _____

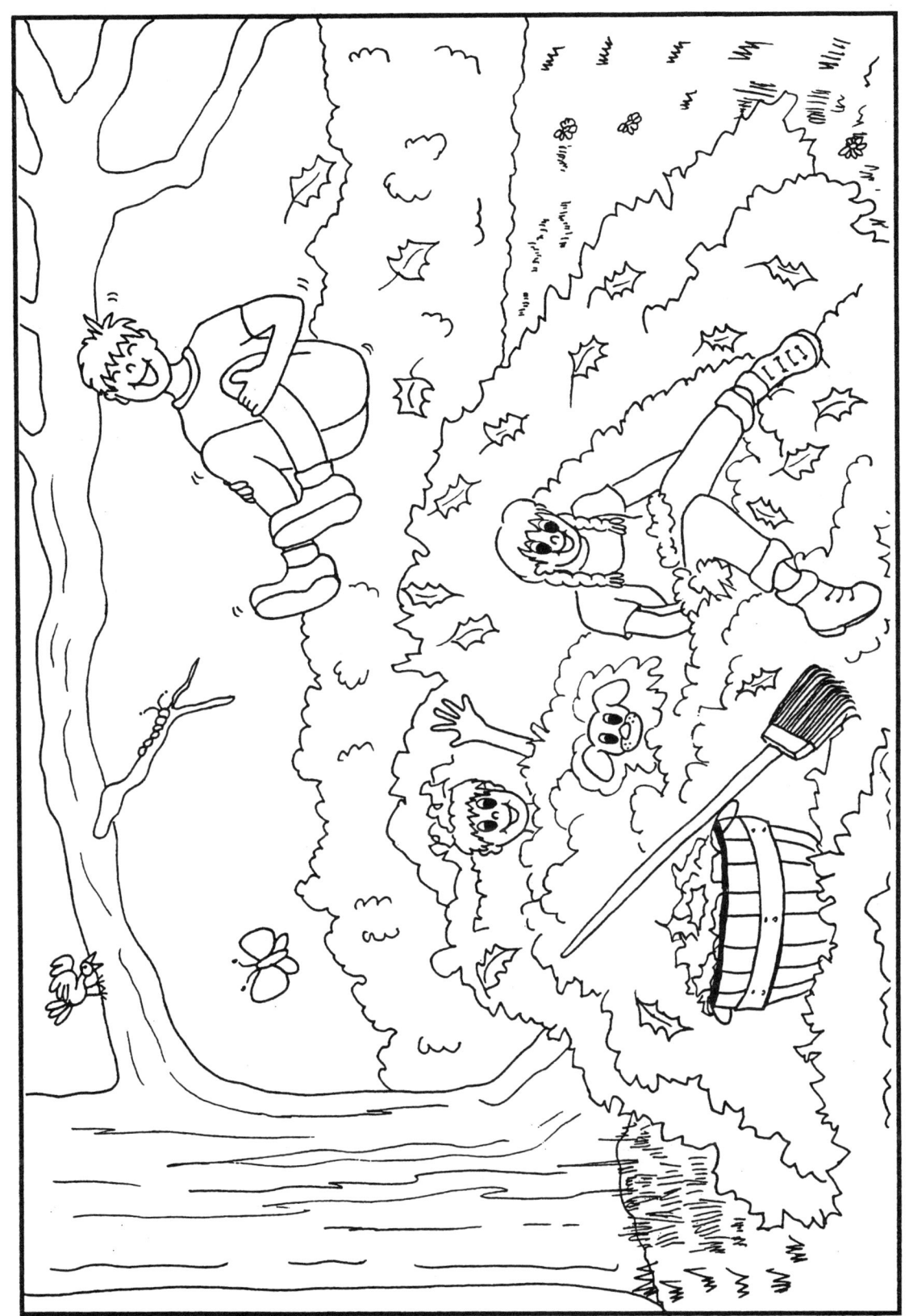

Great Ideas for Teaching, Inc.

Instructor's Worksheet: The purpose of this activity is to help students understand and remember the general meaning and specific details of each story.

Directions: Before beginning, cut out small colored-paper squares to use in the **Following Directions** activities. Each student should be given two squares each of blue, red, yellow and green paper and one copy of the large picture. The instructor will read the story aloud while the students look at their large picture. The students should touch the people and objects in the picture as the story is being read if this aids them in remembering the information. Next, the instructor will read each activity aloud, allowing adequate time for the students to complete each task. When placing a paper square, the students should shield their papers until everyone has finished and then uncover their papers to see if everyone has used the same color and put it in the same place. When answering questions, students should take turns answering the questions aloud. Remembering names may be difficult. The students may need these names reviewed as the questions continue.

Story:

Pam, Chris and Bob were raking up leaves in Bob's backyard. Their pile of leaves was getting higher and higher. Chris was the first to jump into the pile and now he is under most of the leaves. Pam's dog is in the middle of the leaves with him. Pam just fell backwards into the leaves. Bob has taken a big jump and is just about to fall into the leaves. They look like they are having a great time. It is October, when leaves start to fall, but it must be a warm day because all of the children have on shirts with short sleeves.

Auditory Processing for General Comprehension:

1. What are the children doing?
2. Are their parents helping?
3. Who was the first to jump into the leaves?
4. Who fell backwards into the leaves?
5. How can you tell the weather is not cold?

Auditory Processing for Following Directions:

1. Put a yellow square on Chris's hair.
2. Draw a circle around something that is crawling.
3. Put two dots on two things that have wings.
4. Put a red square on the person who fell backwards.
5. Put a green square on someone who isn't in the leaves yet.

Auditory Processing and Sentence Completion:

1. Chris was the first to jump into the _____.
2. Pam fell backwards into the _____.
3. Some of the leaves are in a round _____.
4. They were piling up the leaves with a _____.
5. Two things have wings; a butterfly and a _____.

Auditory Processing and Remembering Specific Information:

1. What is the name of the girl?
2. Who is not in the leaves yet?
3. Who was the first to jump into the leaves?
4. What tool were they using?
5. Do you remember in what month this is happening?

Name: _____

Great Ideas for Teaching, Inc.

Instructor's Worksheet:

The purpose of this activity is to help students understand and remember the general meaning and specific details of each story.

Directions: Before beginning, cut out small colored-paper squares to use in the **Following Directions** activities. Each student should be given two squares each of blue, red, yellow and green paper and one copy of the large picture. The instructor will read the story aloud while the students look at their large picture. The students should touch the people and objects in the picture as the story is being read if this aids them in remembering the information. Next, the instructor will read each activity aloud, allowing adequate time for the students to complete each task. When placing a paper square, the students should shield their papers until everyone has finished and then uncover their papers to see if everyone has used the same color and put it in the same place. When answering questions, students should take turns answering the questions aloud. Remembering names may be difficult. The students may need these names reviewed as the questions continue.

Story:

Kevin and Marla are brother and sister. They are the two children who are just jumping off the pier. Their last name is Smith. Chris and Pam are also brother and sister. Their last name is Jones. Their two families are on vacation together at White Lake. The little dog is named Spot and it belongs to Pam. You can tell all the children know how to swim. If they did not know how to swim, they would stay close to the edge of the water and not jump off the pier. You can see their towels on the pier. The pier is made of wood. There is a ladder to climb at the end of the pier, but you cannot see it in the picture because it is between the two pilings that hold the pier. The two posts at the end of the pier that go down into the water are called pilings.

Auditory Processing for General Comprehension:

1. What are the children doing?
2. Where are they?
3. Is this where the families live all year? Explain.
4. How do you know the children can swim?
5. Describe the pier.

Auditory Processing for Following Directions:

1. Put a yellow square on each of the two children whose last name is Smith.
2. You can see Pam just hitting the water. Circle her brother's hand.
3. Put a blue square on each of the pilings.
4. Make a small circle on the thing that lets you know it is a sunny day.
5. Put a line under a family pet.

Auditory Processing and Sentence Completion:

1. Spot is running and jumping on the _____.
2. Chris is already in the _____.
3. All the children know how to _____.
4. The pier is made of _____.
5. After they swim, they will dry off with their _____.

Auditory Processing and Remembering Specific Information:

1. Point to Kevin's sister. What is her name?
2. What is the dog's name?
3. Is White Lake where they live or where they are vacationing?
4. Where is the ladder that you cannot see?
5. What are the names of the two boys?

Name: _____

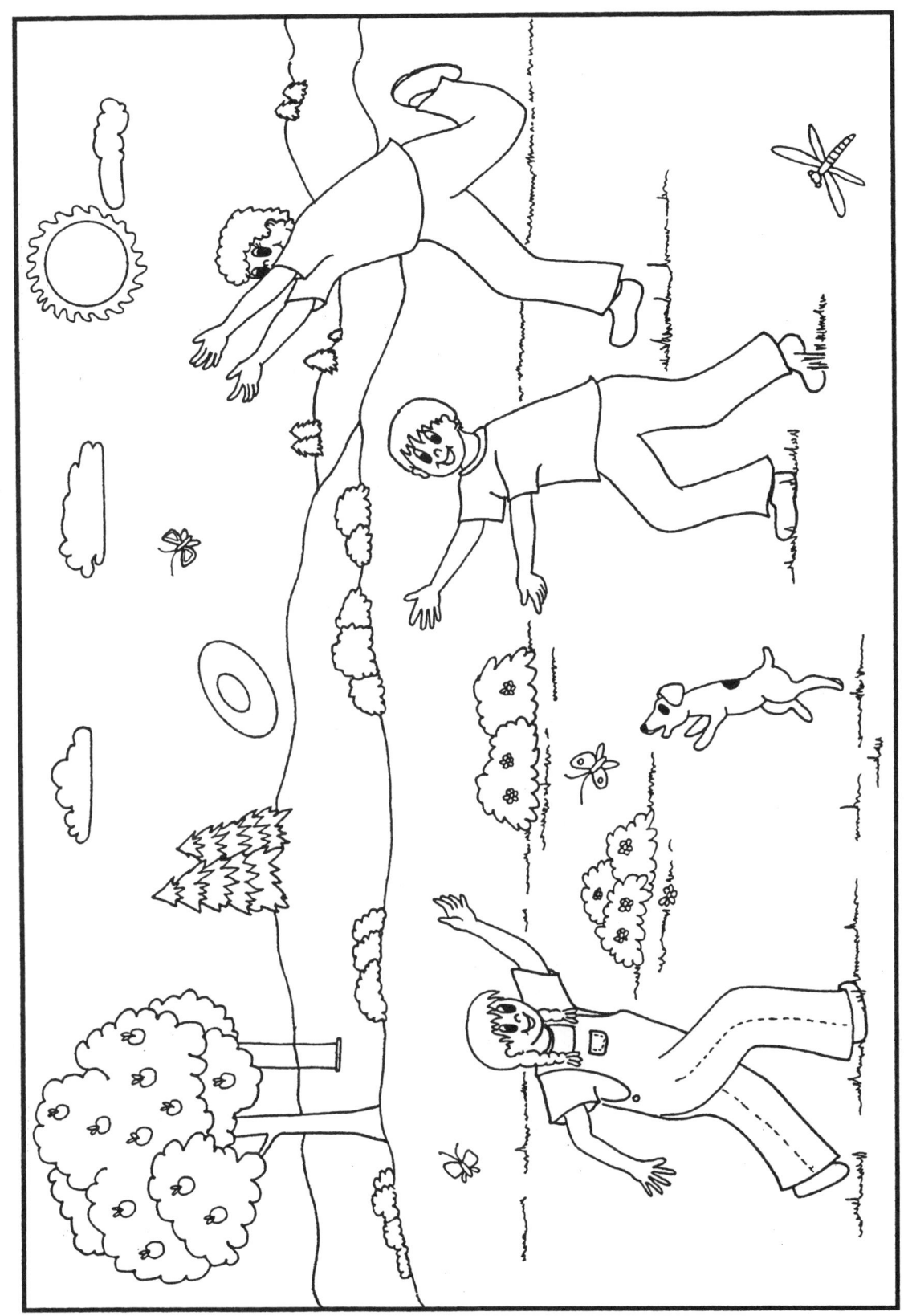

Great Ideas for Teaching, Inc.

Instructor's Worksheet: The purpose of this activity is to help students understand and remember the general meaning and specific details of each story.

Directions: Before beginning, cut out small colored-paper squares to use in the **Following Directions** activities. Each student should be given two squares each of blue, red, yellow and green paper and one copy of the large picture. The instructor will read the story aloud while the students look at their large picture. The students should touch the people and objects in the picture as the story is being read if this aids them in remembering the information. Next, the instructor will read each activity aloud, allowing adequate time for the students to complete each task. When placing a paper square, the students should shield their papers until everyone has finished and then uncover their papers to see if everyone has used the same color and put it in the same place. When answering questions, students should take turns answering the questions aloud. Remembering names may be difficult. The students may need these names reviewed as the questions continue.

Story:

Pam, Chris and Sam are out in the yard throwing a Frisbee. Spot, Pam's dog, is outside playing with the children but he is also busy trying to catch butterflies. It is a beautiful summer day and the weather is very warm. Pam is trying to toss the Frisbee to Chris but it flies right over his head and Sam is running to catch it instead. Chris has his arms up but it is so high he cannot possibly reach it. Sam is older and taller than the other two children so it probably will not go over his head. There is a little butterfly near the Frisbee. It will flutter out of the way just in time not to get hit.

Auditory Processing for General Comprehension:

1. What are the children doing?
2. What is their dog Spot doing?
3. What kind of weather is it?
4. Did the Frisbee go where Pam meant to throw it?
5. Is anyone going to catch it?

Auditory Processing for Following Directions:

1. Put a green square on the Frisbee.
2. Put a blue square on the person who was supposed to catch it.
3. Put an "X" on the person who will probably catch the Frisbee.
4. Count the butterflies and write that number in between Pam and Spot.
5. Circle two apples on the apple tree.

Auditory Processing and Sentence Completion:

1. The children are throwing a _____.
2. Spot is trying to catch a _____.
3. The Frisbee flew over Chris's _____.
4. The Frisbee almost hit a _____.
5. The fruit tree has lots of _____.

Auditory Processing and Remembering Specific Information:

1. What is the name of the girl?
2. Where is this happening?
3. What is Spot trying to catch?
4. Who will try to catch the Frisbee?
5. Is it summer or fall?

Name: _____

Instructor's Worksheet: The purpose of this activity is to help students understand and remember the general meaning and specific details of each story.

Directions: Before beginning, cut out small colored-paper squares to use in the **Following Directions** activities. Each student should be given two squares each of blue, red, yellow and green paper and one copy of the large picture. The instructor will read the story aloud while the students look at their large picture. The students should touch the people and objects in the picture as the story is being read if this aids them in remembering the information. Next, the instructor will read each activity aloud, allowing adequate time for the students to complete each task. When placing a paper square, the students should shield their papers until everyone has finished and then uncover their papers to see if everyone has used the same color and put it in the same place. When answering questions, students should take turns answering the questions aloud. Remembering names may be difficult. The students may need these names reviewed as the questions continue.

Story:

Pam, Rick, and Chris took a walk to the pond that is near their houses. They knew the large swan in the pond was sitting on a nest with eggs and they wanted to see if the eggs had hatched yet. They are so excited. The mother swan is in the water and she has three babies with her. The babies are so tiny that they look like little floating fuzzy toys. Pam said, "I brought some bread with me. I will break the bread in really small pieces and see if the babies can eat the crumbs." The mother swan and the babies seem very excited and are swimming over for the treats. The tall plants at the edge of the water are called cattails. Can you remember that? They certainly do not look like the tails of cats.

Auditory Processing for General Comprehension:

1. Where did the children walk?
2. What do they see in the water?
3. What was the mother swan doing the last time the children were at the pond?
4. What did Pam bring with her?
5. What is she doing with the bread?

Auditory Processing for Following Directions:

1. Put a small "X" on the mother in the story.
2. Put a number 1 on each of the swan's babies.
3. Circle two of the cattails.
4. Put a yellow square on one of Pam's arms.
5. Put a blue square on each of the children who did not bring bread.

Auditory Processing and Sentence Completion:

1. The last time the children were at the pond, the swan was sitting on a _____.
2. Today, the babies are in the _____.
3. The baby swans hatched out of the _____.
4. Pam remembered to bring along some _____.
5. She broke the bread into little _____.

Auditory Processing and Remembering Specific Information:

1. What is the name of the girl?
2. Listen to these four names and say which two are the names of the boys in the story? Roger, Chris, Rick, Stanley.
3. What are the tall plants growing at the edge of the water?
4. Does the swan have her babies in a river or in a pond?
5. Are these baby swans or baby ducks?

Name: _____

Auditory Processing of Early
Language Comprehension Skills

Great Ideas for Teaching, Inc.

Instructor's Worksheet: The purpose of this activity is to help students understand and remember the general meaning and specific details of each story.

Directions: Before beginning, cut out small colored-paper squares to use in the **Following Directions** activities. Each student should be given two squares each of blue, red, yellow and green paper and one copy of the large picture. The instructor will read the story aloud while the students look at their large picture. The students should touch the people and objects in the picture as the story is being read if this aids them in remembering the information. Next, the instructor will read each activity aloud, allowing adequate time for the students to complete each task. When placing a paper square, the students should shield their papers until everyone has finished and then uncover their papers to see if everyone has used the same color and put it in the same place. When answering questions, students should take turns answering the questions aloud. Remembering names may be difficult. The students may need these names reviewed as the questions continue.

Story:

Here you see Chris, Pam and Rick again. Someone gave the children a big bag of balloons. They have been blowing up balloons for the last three days. They have so many balloons that they don't know what to do with them. Chris said, "Why don't we teach our dog some tricks? Then we can decorate our porch with all the balloons and have a dog show. We can invite all of the children in the neighborhood and give them a balloon to take home." Pam and Rick thought that was a great idea. Today is the day of the dog show. They are using Chris's porch since it was his idea. They have dressed their dogs up in costumes and their pets are doing tricks. Everyone is having a good time. They will give each person a balloon when the show is over.

Auditory Processing for General Comprehension:

1. What did someone give to the children?
2. What have they been doing for the last three days?
3. What did Chris suggest that they do?
4. Who will do the tricks in the show?
5. What will they give each person at the end of the show?

Auditory Processing for Following Directions:

1. Put a small "X" on two of the things that someone gave the children?
2. Chris is the boy on the left. Put a blue square on him.
3. Rick is the boy on the right. Put a red square on his shirt.
4. Put an "X" on the shoulder of the boy who suggested the dog show.
5. Put a green square on each of the pets.

Auditory Processing and Sentence Completion:

1. Someone gave the children a bag of _____.
2. They have been blowing up balloons for three _____.
3. Chris thought it would be fun to have a _____.
4. They decorated Chris's porch with _____.
5. When the children leave, each will be given a _____.

Auditory Processing and Remembering Specific Information:

1. What are the names of the three children?
2. Where are they having the show?
3. What are the decorations?
4. What is the entertainment?
5. What will the neighborhood children take home?

Name: _____

Great Ideas for Teaching, Inc.

Instructor's Worksheet: The purpose of this activity is to help students understand and remember the general meaning and specific details of each story.

Directions: Before beginning, cut out small colored-paper squares to use in the **Following Directions** activities. Each student should be given two squares each of blue, red, yellow and green paper and one copy of the large picture. The instructor will read the story aloud while the students look at their large picture. The students should touch the people and objects in the picture as the story is being read if this aids them in remembering the information. Next, the instructor will read each activity aloud, allowing adequate time for the students to complete each task. When placing a paper square, the students should shield their papers until everyone has finished and then uncover their papers to see if everyone has used the same color and put it in the same place. When answering questions, students should take turns answering the questions aloud. Remembering names may be difficult. The students may need these names reviewed as the questions continue.

Story:

Today is Rick's birthday. He is having a birthday party in his backyard. His two best friends, Pam and Chris are there. They live on the farm next to Rick's farm. That is Pam's dog Spot jumping up and down. Rick's mom ordered a very special pinata for his birthday. A pinata is a big paper container that is filled with all types of candy. Pam is wearing a blindfold and is trying to hit it to break it open. They take turns trying to break it open. The last time Pam had a turn, she knocked off Rick's hat, rather than hit the pinata. This time she was lucky and made the first hole in the pinata and some of the candy fell out. It is Rick's turn next. Do you think he will hit it and make the hole bigger? He hopes so! Later, they are going to have ice cream and cake. They are having a great time!

Auditory Processing for General Comprehension:

1. What is special about today?
2. Where are they having a party?
3. What did Rick's mother order?
4. What did Pam hit earlier?
5. What did Pam hit this time?

Auditory Processing and Separating Information:

1. Whose birthday is it?
2. Where do Rick and his friends live?
3. Who brought a dog along?
4. What did Pam hit on her first try?
5. What is inside the pinata?

Auditory Processing and Sentence Completion:

1. Today is Rick's _____.
2. His party is in his _____.
3. His mother ordered a special birthday _____.
4. The first person to make a hole in the pinata was _____.
5. Later, Rick's mother will serve _____.

Auditory Processing and Retelling Information:

1. Tell what is special about today.
2. Describe the decorations for the party.
3. Describe a pinata.
4. Pam has had two turns. Describe both of them.
5. Tell what Rick hopes will happen when he takes the next turn.

Auditory Processing of Early
Language Comprehension Skills

Name: _____

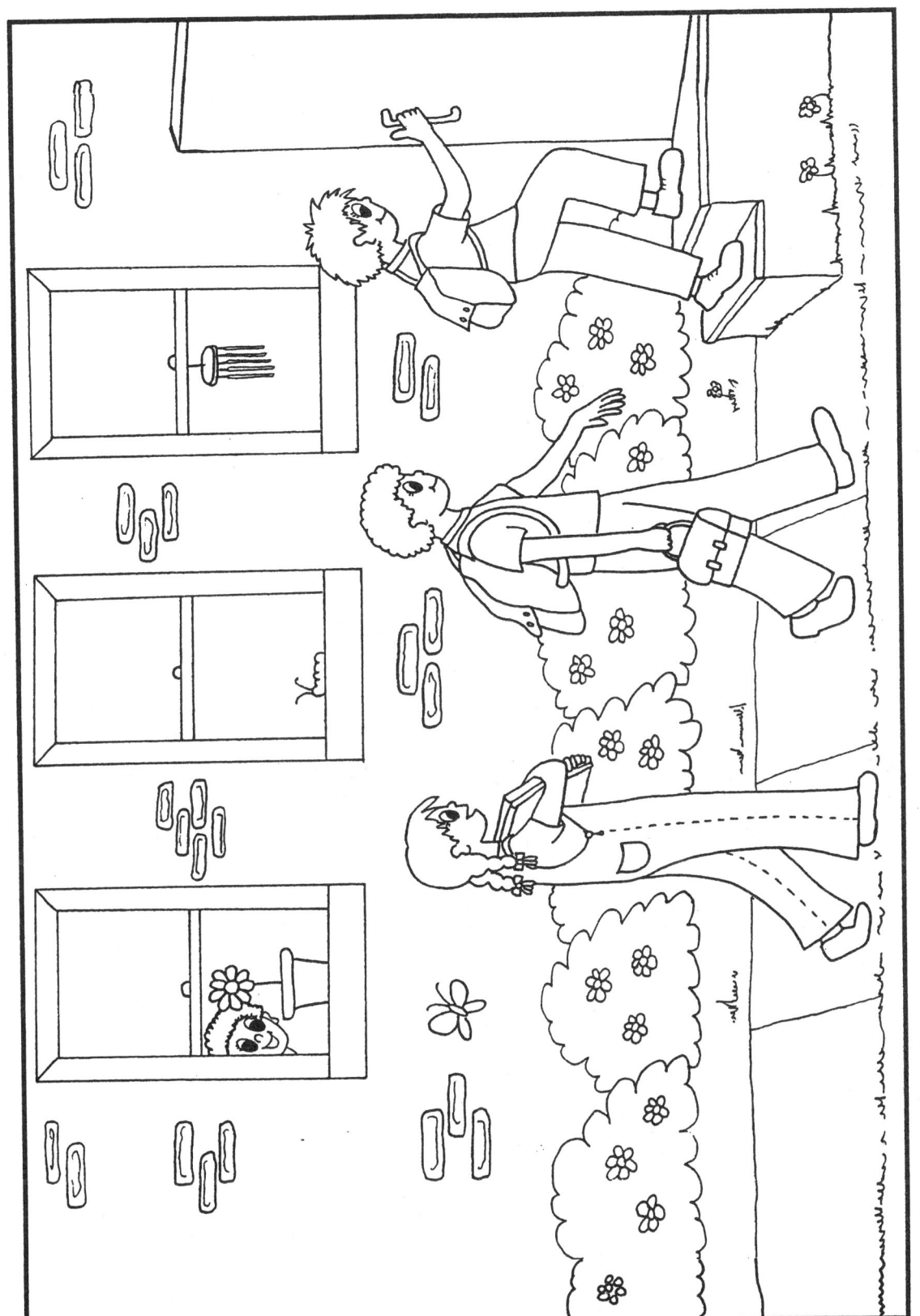

Auditory Processing of Early
Language Comprehension Skills

Great Ideas for Teaching, Inc.

Instructor's Worksheet: The purpose of this activity is to help students understand and remember the general meaning and specific details of each story.

Directions: Before beginning, cut out small colored-paper squares to use in the **Following Directions** activities. Each student should be given two squares each of blue, red, yellow and green paper and one copy of the large picture. The instructor will read the story aloud while the students look at their large picture. The students should touch the people and objects in the picture as the story is being read if this aids them in remembering the information. Next, the instructor will read each activity aloud, allowing adequate time for the students to complete each task. When placing a paper square, the students should shield their papers until everyone has finished and then uncover their papers to see if everyone has used the same color and put it in the same place. When answering questions, students should take turns answering the questions aloud. Remembering names may be difficult. The students may need these names reviewed as the questions continue.

Story:

Today is Monday and all the children are going to school. Pam, Chris and Rick rode the school bus to school and now they are walking to their classroom. All of them are in the same class this year. That is very nice because they are all best friends. Now they will be able to do homework together if they want to. All three of them really like school and they all make very good grades. Pam wants to be a famous writer some day. She loves English. That is her favorite subject. Chris likes science and is always catching bugs, hunting unusual rocks and things like that. Rick loves math. He is always the first one finished on all the math tests. Their teacher always praises him and tells him he is the Math Wizard of the school. He wants to be a math teacher one day.

Auditory Processing for General Comprehension:

1. Where are the children going?
2. Are they the first to arrive?
3. How did they get to school?
4. How do they feel about school?
5. Do all three children like the same subject best?

Auditory Processing and Separating Information:

1. Why will they probably see a lot of each other this year?
2. Which child gets praised as a Math Wizard?
3. Who likes everything about science?
4. Who hopes to be a famous writer?
5. How do the children get to school?

Auditory Processing and Sentence Completion:

1. Pam wants to be a famous _____.
2. Chris always likes to collect _____.
3. Rick is the first one finished on all the _____.
4. They are all in the same _____.
5. They are also best _____.

Auditory Processing and Retelling Information:

1. Talk about how the children get to school.
2. Talk about things they have in common.
3. Talk about things they can do together this year.
4. Talk about the subject each one likes best.
5. Talk about what kind of students they are.

Name: _____

Instructor's Worksheet: The purpose of this activity is to help students understand and remember the general meaning and specific details of each story.

Directions: Before beginning, cut out small colored-paper squares to use in the **Following Directions** activities. Each student should be given two squares each of blue, red, yellow and green paper and one copy of the large picture. The instructor will read the story aloud while the students look at their large picture. The students should touch the people and objects in the picture as the story is being read if this aids them in remembering the information. Next, the instructor will read each activity aloud, allowing adequate time for the students to complete each task. When placing a paper square, the students should shield their papers until everyone has finished and then uncover their papers to see if everyone has used the same color and put it in the same place. When answering questions, students should take turns answering the questions aloud. Remembering names may be difficult. The students may need these names reviewed as the questions continue.

Story:

Pam and Chris are sister and brother. Rick is their next door neighbor. They live on farms that are next to each other. They play together all the time when they are not helping with chores around their farms. Chris and Rick started building kites from kits. Pam decided she wanted to build one, also. They glued wood pieces of the frame together, painted their kites, attached all the strings, and tied bows on the tail of each kite to weigh the bottom down. The children painted different pictures on their kites. Rick painted lightning so his would look powerful. Chris painted a face so his would look scary, and Pam painted a butterfly because they know how to fly. Today is the big test to see if they can get their kites to fly. It is the first windy day they have had all summer. Look! Rick already has his kite in the air.

Auditory Processing for General Comprehension:

1. What is different about the weather today?
2. What are the children trying to do?
3. Where did they get the kites?
4. Why are bows tied to the tail of the kites?
5. Why is the dog excited?

Auditory Processing and Separating Information:

1. Which two children started building the kites first?
2. What is the frame of the kite made of?
3. Why did they tie long strings to the kites?
4. Why do they roll the string around a stick?
5. Whose kite is already in the air?

Auditory Processing and Sentence Completion:

1. Chris and Rick were the first to start making _____.
2. Pam told them she also wanted to _____.
3. They carved the pieces for the frame out of _____.
4. They tied bows on the _____.
5. They had been waiting for the weather to be _____.

Auditory Processing and Retelling Information:

1. Tell why Rick wanted to have lightning on his kite.
2. Tell why Pam wanted a butterfly on her kite.
3. Tell why Chris wanted a face on his kite.
4. Tell why they chose today to test their kites.
5. Tell why you think the dog is so excited.

Auditory Processing of Early
Language Comprehension Skills

Name: _____

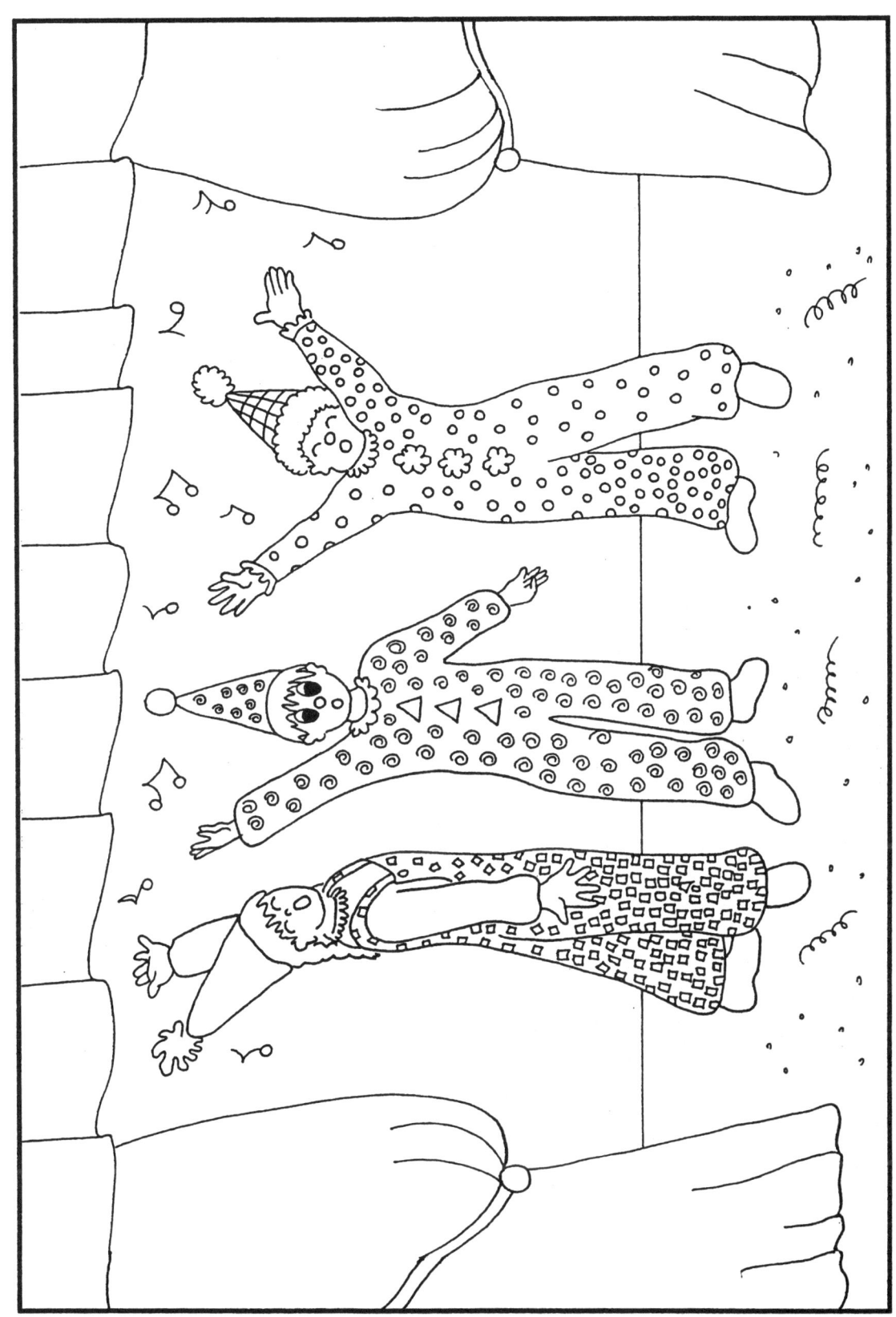

Auditory Processing of Early
Language Comprehension Skills

Great Ideas for Teaching, Inc.

Instructor's Worksheet:
The purpose of this activity is to help students understand and remember the general meaning and specific details of each story.

Directions: Before beginning, cut out small colored-paper squares to use in the **Following Directions** activities. Each student should be given two squares each of blue, red, yellow and green paper and one copy of the large picture. The instructor will read the story aloud while the students look at their large picture. The students should touch the people and objects in the picture as the story is being read if this aids them in remembering the information. Next, the instructor will read each activity aloud, allowing adequate time for the students to complete each task. When placing a paper square, the students should shield their papers until everyone has finished and then uncover their papers to see if everyone has used the same color and put it in the same place. When answering questions, students should take turns answering the questions aloud. Remembering names may be difficult. The students may need these names reviewed as the questions continue.

Story:

Today is the school talent show. Pam, Chris and Rick decided to be in it. Pam is the child on the left. Chris, her brother, is in the middle and their best friend Rick is on the right. They have been practicing for about two weeks. They are dressed up like clowns because they had clown outfits left over from last Halloween. They made up a song called, "I Like Being a Clown." Lots and lots of children are in the talent show. Some dance, some sing, some do tricks, and others just do anything they think will be funny. The children are on stage now. Pam and Rick are singing and moving about. Poor Chris has suddenly forgotten all the words and he cannot even move. Everyone watching the show thinks it is part of their act and that he is so funny. They clap and clap and award them a prize.

Auditory Processing for General Comprehension:

1. What is the school having today?
2. Who are the people on the stage?
3. Where did they get their costumes?
4. What did they decide to do for the talent show?
5. Is the name of their song, "I Like Being a Clown" or "Take Me Out to the Ballgame?"

Auditory Processing and Separating Information:

1. Who remembered the words to the song?
2. Who forgot the words?
3. Did Chris sing the words?
4. Did Rick sing the words?
5. Did Pam both dance and sing?

Auditory Processing and Sentence Completion:

1. The children decided to be in the _____.
2. They made up a song called _____.
3. Chris forgot the words of the _____.
4. Chris is so nervous he can not even _____.
5. The people _____.

Auditory Processing and Retelling Information:

1. Describe what they decided to do in the talent show.
2. Describe where the costumes came from.
3. Describe what happened to Chris.
4. Describe what the people thought about Chris not singing.
5. Describe how a bad thing turned out to be a good thing.

Auditory Processing of Early
Language Comprehension Skills

Name: _____

SNACK BAR

Great Ideas for Teaching, Inc.

Instructor's Worksheet: The purpose of this activity is to help students understand and remember the general meaning and specific details of each story.

<u>Directions:</u> Before beginning, cut out small colored-paper squares to use in the **Following Directions** activities. Each student should be given two squares each of blue, red, yellow and green paper and one copy of the large picture. The instructor will read the story aloud while the students look at their large picture. The students should touch the people and objects in the picture as the story is being read if this aids them in remembering the information. Next, the instructor will read each activity aloud, allowing adequate time for the students to complete each task. When placing a paper square, the students should shield their papers until everyone has finished and then uncover their papers to see if everyone has used the same color and put it in the same place. When answering questions, students should take turns answering the questions aloud. Remembering names may be difficult. The students may need these names reviewed as the questions continue.

Story:

You see Rick, Pam and Chris at the Snack Bar. It is one of their favorite places. Pam and Chris are sister and brother. Rick is their best friend. Their farms are very close to town and it is not too far if they decide to walk. Their parents drove into town today and they rode along. Their parents are at a town meeting. They suggested to the children that today would be a perfect day for them to go to the Snack Bar while their parents are at the meeting. Rick loves hamburgers. He is having a hamburger, french fries and a glass of grape drink. Pam decided to have her favorite thing, a chocolate milkshake. Chris ordered the giant triple-decker ice cream float with whipped cream on top. His float has three kinds of ice cream - chocolate, vanilla and strawberry. You are looking at three very happy children.

Auditory Processing for General Comprehension:

1. Where are the children?
2. Why are they there today?
3. How did they get to town?
4. Did they all order the same thing?
5. Explain how you know they do not mind that their parents had to go to a meeting.

Auditory Processing and Separating Information:

1. Which child preferred not to have something too sweet?
2. Which child preferred to have everything be chocolate?
3. Which child has a brother there?
4. Which child loves lots of flavors of ice cream?
5. Who will take their money for the food?

Auditory Processing and Sentence Completion:

1. The hamburger was ordered by _____.
2. Pam ordered a _____.
3. Their parents are at a _____.
4. Today, they rode to _____.
5. On the top of Chris's ice cream float is _____.

Auditory Processing and Retelling Information:

1. Describe Chris's ice cream float.
2. Describe what Rick ordered.
3. Describe Pam's milkshake.
4. Tell two ways that the children can get to town.
5. Describe where the children live.

Name: _____

Great Ideas for Teaching, Inc.

Instructor's Worksheet: The purpose of this activity is to help students understand and remember the general meaning and specific details of each story.

<u>Directions:</u> Before beginning, cut out small colored-paper squares to use in the **Following Directions** activities. Each student should be given two squares each of blue, red, yellow and green paper and one copy of the large picture. The instructor will read the story aloud while the students look at their large picture. The students should touch the people and objects in the picture as the story is being read if this aids them in remembering the information. Next, the instructor will read each activity aloud, allowing adequate time for the students to complete each task. When placing a paper square, the students should shield their papers until everyone has finished and then uncover their papers to see if everyone has used the same color and put it in the same place. When answering questions, students should take turns answering the questions aloud. Remembering names may be difficult. The students may need these names reviewed as the questions continue.

Story:

Pam, Chris and Rick are in the school lunch room. Their friend Ted is behind them. Chris is first in line. He ordered a slice of pizza and a carton of milk. Pam and Rick are talking. They both want macaroni and cheese, but they haven't ordered yet. Ted brought his lunch in a lunchbox. He just wants to buy milk. The food is always good in the cafeteria, but sometimes the children like to bring their favorite sandwiches from home. They always order milk and sometimes they buy ice cream.

Auditory Processing for General Comprehension:

1. Where are the children?
2. Do they always buy lunch?
3. What are Pam and Rick ordering today?
4. What do they buy each day?
5. Chris already has his plate. What did he order?

Auditory Processing and Separating Information:

1. What are Pam and Rick going to order?
2. What does their friend Ted plan to order?
3. Pam and Chris are sister and brother. Did they order the same thing?
4. Who is last in line and what will he order?
5. Who was the first to order in their group?

Auditory Processing and Sentence Completion:

1. The children are in the school _____.
2. Even if they bring their lunches, they always order _____.
3. Pam and Rick plan to order _____.
4. Chris ordered _____.
5. Sometimes they like a treat and order _____.

Auditory Processing and Retelling Information:

1. What did Chris say when he ordered his lunch?
2. If Pam orders for both herself and Rick, what will she say?
3. What will Ted say when he gets to the counter?
4. What did the story say about how often the children order milk?
5. Tell why Ted is not ordering lunch.

Name: _____

Great Ideas for Teaching, Inc.

Instructor's Worksheet: The purpose of this activity is to help students understand and remember the general meaning and specific details of each story.

Directions: Before beginning, cut out small colored-paper squares to use in the **Following Directions** activities. Each student should be given two squares each of blue, red, yellow and green paper and one copy of the large picture. The instructor will read the story aloud while the students look at their large picture. The students should touch the people and objects in the picture as the story is being read if this aids them in remembering the information. Next, the instructor will read each activity aloud, allowing adequate time for the students to complete each task. When placing a paper square, the students should shield their papers until everyone has finished and then uncover their papers to see if everyone has used the same color and put it in the same place. When answering questions, students should take turns answering the questions aloud. Remembering names may be difficult. The students may need these names reviewed as the questions continue.

Story:

Pam, Chris and Rick have gone to the bakery to buy a special treat. Pam's dog Spot is with them. At first, the baker did not notice Spot. When he did, he told Pam she would need to take her dog outside because pets were not allowed in the bakery. Pam had forgotten that this was the rule in the bakery. You can tell that Spot is certainly enjoying being there. He hopes someone will buy him a treat, also. Pam is asking her brother to buy her one of the frosted cookies on the top shelf in the glass cabinet because she needs to take Spot outside. She is sure both of the boys will want chocolate brownies for themselves. They won't need to share with Spot because Spot gets sick from chocolate.

Auditory Processing for General Comprehension:

1. Where are the children?
2. Why have they gone there?
3. Did the baker notice Spot when the children first came in?
4. When the baker saw Spot, what did he say?
5. What is Pam going to do?

Auditory Processing and Separating Information:

1. Who wants a frosted cookie?
2. What flavor can Spot not eat?
3. Who told Pam that dogs are not allowed in the bakery?
4. Who wants chocolate brownies?
5. Who will share with Spot?

Auditory Processing and Sentence Completion:

1. The children went to the _____.
2. At first, the baker did not notice _____.
3. He told Pam that dogs are not allowed in the _____.
4. Pam asked her brother to buy her a frosted _____.
5. Both of the boys will probably buy chocolate _____.

Auditory Processing and Retelling Information:

1. What did the baker tell Pam?
2. What does Pam need to do with Spot?
3. Tell what she said to her brother as she went outside.
4. Describe what the two boys love best in the bakery.
5. Tell why Spot cannot eat chocolate.

Name: _____

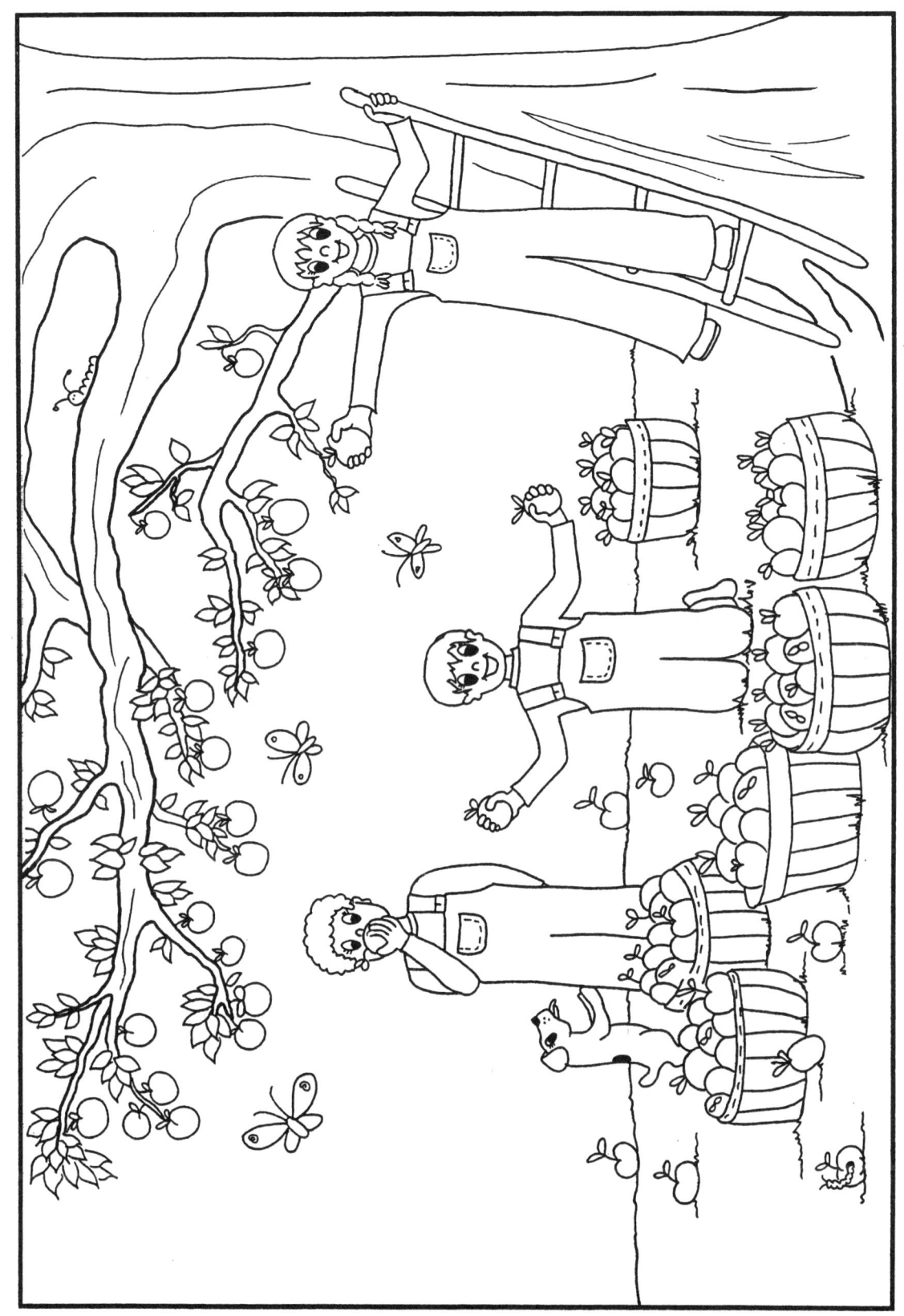

Instructor's Worksheet:
The purpose of this activity is to help students understand and remember the general meaning and specific details of each story.

<u>Directions:</u> Before beginning, cut out small colored-paper squares to use in the **Following Directions** activities. Each student should be given two squares each of blue, red, yellow and green paper and one copy of the large picture. The instructor will read the story aloud while the students look at their large picture. The students should touch the people and objects in the picture as the story is being read if this aids them in remembering the information. Next, the instructor will read each activity aloud, allowing adequate time for the students to complete each task. When placing a paper square, the students should shield their papers until everyone has finished and then uncover their papers to see if everyone has used the same color and put it in the same place. When answering questions, students should take turns answering the questions aloud. Remembering names may be difficult. The students may need these names reviewed as the questions continue.

Story:

Chris and Pam live on a farm. Rick is their next door neighbor. He lives on a farm also. Chris and Pam asked their parents if they could pick apples and sell them at the fruit and vegetable stand their family owns. Their parents thought that would be a fine idea and they could earn money all by themselves. They asked their friend Rick if he would like to do it with them. He was very happy to join them because the children are best friends and play together all the time. You can see in the picture that the apple tree is full of apples, so it is easy to pick a lot of them. Some have already fallen on the ground. They will not use them unless they are in perfect shape with no bruises from falling on the ground.

Auditory Processing for General Comprehension:

1. What good idea did Chris and Pam think of?
2. What kind of tree will they need to climb?
3. What do they plan to do with the apples?
4. Who is going to help them?
5. Where do these children live?

Auditory Processing for Following Directions:

1. Put a yellow square on each of the two children who live on this farm.
2. Put an blue square on the shoulder of their next door neighbor.
3. Circle the apple that no one wants to eat.
4. Draw a line under all of the butterflies.
5. Put a green square on the tree trunk.

Auditory Processing and Sentence Completion:

1. Today, Chris and Pam thought of a great _____.
2. They wanted to pick apples to _____.
3. Their next-door friend is named _____.
4. They put all the apples in _____.
5. There are still lots of apples left on the _____.

Auditory Processing and Remembering Specific Information:

1. What are the names of the three children?
2. Who lives on this farm?
3. Where does Rick live?
4. Where will they sell the apples?
5. How many baskets of apples have they picked?

Auditory Processing of Early
Language Comprehension Skills

Name: _____

Great Ideas for Teaching, Inc.

Instructor's Worksheet:
The purpose of this activity is to help students understand and remember the general meaning and specific details of each story.

Directions: Before beginning, cut out small colored-paper squares to use in the **Following Directions** activities. Each student should be given two squares each of blue, red, yellow and green paper and one copy of the large picture. The instructor will read the story aloud while the students look at their large picture. The students should touch the people and objects in the picture as the story is being read if this aids them in remembering the information. Next, the instructor will read each activity aloud, allowing adequate time for the students to complete each task. When placing a paper square, the students should shield their papers until everyone has finished and then uncover their papers to see if everyone has used the same color and put it in the same place. When answering questions, students should take turns answering the questions aloud. Remembering names may be difficult. The students may need these names reviewed as the questions continue.

Story:

Pam, Chris and Rick are visiting a pet store today. The store is having an "open-house" which means everyone is invited to visit the store today. Pam's dog Spot is with them. The store owner does not mind Spot visiting the pet store because he has such good manners and is so well-behaved. He never barks in the store and stays right beside the children all the time. Today, Spot and Pam are watching the parrot. The parrot is new and is supposed to be able to talk but it hasn't said a word yet. Chris is playing with a new litter of puppies. They are very playful. Rick is watching a bunny that is getting ready to eat a carrot. He was afraid the rabbit might fall off the counter but the store owner said the rabbit never tries to get down. They love visiting the pet store. They come here often because it is where they buy Spot's food and treats.

Auditory Processing for General Comprehension:

1. Where are the children?
2. What is the store having today?
3. Are dogs allowed?
4. What is new in the store today?
5. Does the store's owner think the rabbit will fall off the counter?

Auditory Processing for Following Directions:

1. Put a green square on something that is supposed to talk.
2. Put a yellow square on something with large ears.
3. Circle the animal that has good manners and is well-behaved.
4. Put lines under the things that are playful.
5. Put a blue square on the shirt of the person who was afraid the rabbit might get hurt.

Auditory Processing and Sentence Completion:

1. Pam and Spot are looking at the _____.
2. The little puppies are very _____.
3. Pam is waiting to hear the parrot _____.
4. The rabbit likes to stay on the _____.
5. The store owner thinks their dog has good _____.

Auditory Processing and Remembering Specific Information:

1. Today there is an "open-house" at the _____.
2. The new pet is a parrot that can _____.
3. The rabbit is sitting on the _____.
4. Chris is playing with the _____.
5. The children come here often to buy _____.

Name: _____

Auditory Processing of Early
Language Comprehension Skills

Great Ideas for Teaching, Inc.

Instructor's Worksheet: The purpose of this activity is to help students understand and remember the general meaning and specific details of each story.

<u>Directions:</u> Before beginning, cut out small colored-paper squares to use in the **Following Directions** activities. Each student should be given two squares each of blue, red, yellow and green paper and one copy of the large picture. The instructor will read the story aloud while the students look at their large picture. The students should touch the people and objects in the picture as the story is being read if this aids them in remembering the information. Next, the instructor will read each activity aloud, allowing adequate time for the students to complete each task. When placing a paper square, the students should shield their papers until everyone has finished and then uncover their papers to see if everyone has used the same color and put it in the same place. When answering questions, students should take turns answering the questions aloud. Remembering names may be difficult. The students may need these names reviewed as the questions continue.

Story:

Today Spot hurt his right front leg when he was chasing a rabbit in the backyard. Someone had left a rake in the yard instead of putting it back in the garage where it belonged. Spot was running too fast to be careful and took a bad tumble. Spot whimpered and couldn't walk on the leg that was hurt. Pam's brother Chris was not home so Pam asked their good friend Rick to go with her to the vet. Pam's mother drove them. The veterinarian took an x-ray of Spot's leg and said it was not broken but that a prong of the rake had cut Spot's leg. He put medicine on the cut and bandaged it. Pam and Rick made Spot feel a lot better. They promised Spot lots of treats when they get home.

Auditory Processing for General Comprehension:

1. What was Spot doing when the accident happened?
2. What did Spot tumble over?
3. Why was the rake on the ground?
4. How did they know Spot needed to go to the vet?
5. What was wrong with Spot's leg?

Auditory Processing and Separating Information:

1. What was Spot chasing?
2. Put a blue square on the leg that was cut.
3. Put a yellow square on the veterinarian.
4. Put a red square on the owner of Spot.
5. How did the veterinarian know Spot's leg was not broken?

Auditory Processing and Sentence Completion:

1. Spot was chasing a _____.
2. Someone had left a rake on the _____.
3. Spot tumbled over the _____.
4. Pam's mother drove them to the _____.
5. How did the veterinarian know Spot's leg was not broken?

Auditory Processing and Retelling Information:

1. Tell why Spot was not being careful.
2. Tell how someone's forgetfulness caused an accident.
3. Tell how Pam knew Spot was hurt.
4. Tell why Rick went with Pam and Spot.
5. Tell what was wrong with Spot.

Name: _____

Great Ideas for Teaching, Inc.

Instructor's Worksheet:
Instructor's Worksheet: The purpose of this activity is to help students understand and remember the general meaning and specific details of each story.

Directions: Before beginning, cut out small colored-paper squares to use in the **Following Directions** activities. Each student should be given two squares each of blue, red, yellow and green paper and one copy of the large picture. The instructor will read the story aloud while the students look at their large picture. The students should touch the people and objects in the picture as the story is being read if this aids them in remembering the information. Next, the instructor will read each activity aloud, allowing adequate time for the students to complete each task. When placing a paper square, the students should shield their papers until everyone has finished and then uncover their papers to see if everyone has used the same color and put it in the same place. When answering questions, students should take turns answering the questions aloud. Remembering names may be difficult. The students may need these names reviewed as the questions continue.

Story:

Pam and Chris are sister and brother. Rick is their best friend. Pam, Chris, and their dog Spot walked over to Rick's house to see if he wanted to go to the movies. Rick told them he couldn't go because he promised his mother he would paint the fence. Pam and Chris offered to help paint. They thought painting would probably be more fun than going to the movies. Everyone was doing a great job painting. No one was really watching their dog because Spot is usually very good and very careful. Not today, it seems. Before anyone could stop him, Spot turned over Rick's paint can. What a mess! As soon as the paint spilled, Rusty decided he had better leave....in a hurry.

Auditory Processing for General Comprehension:

1. Where did Pam and Chris go?
2. Why can't Rick go to the movies?
3. What did Pam and Chris think would be more fun than seeing a movie?
4. Was anyone watching Spot?
5. What did Spot decide to do after turning over the paint can?

Auditory Processing for Separating Information:

1. What did Pam and Chris first want to do?
2. What did they decide would be more fun?
3. Put a yellow square on the person who promised his mother that he would paint the fence.
4. Put a red square on each of the people who brought Spot.
5. Put a blue square on what was knocked over.

Auditory Processing and Sentence Completion:

1. Pam and Chris walked over to see _____.
2. They wanted him to go to the _____.
3. Rick told them he had to paint the _____.
4. Pam and Chris thought it would be more fun to _____.
5. Spot turned over the _____.

Auditory Processing and Retelling Information:

1. Tell why Rick can not go to the movies today.
2. Tell what Pam and Chris decided to do and why.
3. Tell what kind of painting job they were doing.
4. Tell what Spot did when no one was looking.
5. Tell what Spot decided to do after turning over the paint can.

Name: _____

59

Instructor's Worksheet: The purpose of this activity is to help students understand and remember the general meaning and specific details of each story.

<u>Directions:</u> Before beginning, cut out small colored-paper squares to use in the **Following Directions** activities. Each student should be given two squares each of blue, red, yellow and green paper and one copy of the large picture. The instructor will read the story aloud while the students look at their large picture. The students should touch the people and objects in the picture as the story is being read if this aids them in remembering the information. Next, the instructor will read each activity aloud, allowing adequate time for the students to complete each task. When placing a paper square, the students should shield their papers until everyone has finished and then uncover their papers to see if everyone has used the same color and put it in the same place. When answering questions, students should take turns answering the questions aloud. Remembering names may be difficult. The students may need these names reviewed as the questions continue.

Story:

Chris is in the hospital. He became very ill with a stomach virus and the doctor thought he would be better off in the hospital until his fever was gone and he was better. His sister Pam and his best friend Rick were not allowed to visit him before today. Now he is much better and his fever is all gone. The nurses even let the family pet visit him in hopes that this would make him feel better faster. Rick promised to hold Spot the whole time so Spot would not bother any other patients. Pam brought Chris a pretty plant with a bow on the plant's pot. Rick brought the three balloons that are tied to the top of the chair. You can see that Chris has received other flowers, cards, and balloons. The little box that is hanging over the headboard of the bed has buttons on it. If Chris needs to call a nurse, he pushes one of the buttons.

Auditory Processing for General Comprehension:

1. Where is Chris?
2. Why is he in the hospital?
3. Who decided he should go to the hospital?
4. What did Pam bring to her brother?
5. What did Rick bring to his friend?

Auditory Processing and Separating Information:

1. Put a blue square on the child who is ill.
2. Put a yellow square on the person who promised to take care of Spot during the visit.
3. Who brought the balloons that are tied to the chair?
4. Put a green square on the button Chris pushes to call the nurse.
5. Why are the children finally allowed to visit Chris?

Auditory Processing and Sentence Completion:

1. Chris became ill with a stomach _____.
2. The doctor thought he should go to the _____.
3. Today is the first day the children have been allowed to visit _____.
4. Pam brought her brother a _____.
5. Rick brought the balloons that are tied to the _____.

Auditory Processing and Retelling Information:

1. Tell why Chris had to go to the hospital.
2. Tell why he is finally able to have visitors.
3. Tell why the nurse allowed the family pet to visit Chris.
4. Tell about the other gifts that have been sent to Chris.
5. Tell why Chris has the little box that is hanging over the headboard of his bed.

Auditory Processing of Early
Language Comprehension Skills